CREATING *Positive* RACE RELATIONS

What You Can do to Make a Difference

TAYLOR COX JR.

EDITOR

WESTBOW
PRESS®
A DIVISION OF THOMAS NELSON
& ZONDERVAN

WestBow Press books may be ordered through booksellers or by contacting:

WestBow Press
A Division of Thomas Nelson & Zondervan
1663 Liberty Drive
Bloomington, IN 47403
www.westbowpress.com
844-714-3454

ISBN: 978-1-6642-1065-3 (sc)
ISBN: 978-1-6642-1064-6 (e)

Library of Congress Control Number: 2020921365

Print information available on the last page.

WestBow Press rev. date: 11/19/2020

CONTENTS

INTRODUCTION

Starting in 2018 a mixed-race group of twelve men have gathered monthly in response to persistent racial prejudice and division in our nation and their consequences.

While acknowledging that there has been much progress in race relations, and in the effects of race over the past six decades, we believe significant on-going shortcomings in these areas are among the most spiritually, economically, socially, and emotionally destructive problems that exist in our nation. Specifically, as we observe the current status of race in our nation, we are gravely concerned there is (1) still too much racial segregation; (2) too many instances of young Blacks being killed in interactions with law enforcement officers; (3) too much racial tension; (4) too many wide gaps between races in achievement and opportunities in education, economic well-being, and access to good medical care; and (5) too little unity and collaborative effort among the races toward achieving common goals.

We want to emphasize that people of all races—not just whites as the racial majority—are responsible for the nation's ongoing racial prejudice and division. Therefore, we all need to act to change the status quo. Accordingly, *our mission is to reduce division and improve the quality of interracial relations in our region and nation.*

Specifically, we seek to:

1. Reduce race-related injustices.
2. Improve the ability of people of different racial backgrounds to work collaboratively.
3. Decrease race-related violence.
4. Increase the number of high-quality, one-on-one interracial relationships.

To accomplish our mission, we met with an expert on cultural diversity every month for two years and learned about racial dynamics through dialogue, sharing of personal stories and experiences, and discussion of race-related case studies. We then turned our attention to the following question: **What can we do to improve the quality of interracial relations in our region and beyond?**

After much discussion, we agreed to undertake two actions:

1. Identify and publish a set of steps, or actions, to help people become personal change agents who reduce racial prejudices and promote racial harmony.
2. Engage people in our spheres of influence in learning experiences that promote dialogue and personal development around *positive race relations*—that is, improving race-related issues on each of the four specific goals listed earlier.

This book is the result of the first action. The format is designed to take readers on a journey where they learn about race and how they can make a difference through their future communications and behaviors. It also shares what our group members learned over the past two years of collaboration.

We recognize that because our group consists only of Blacks and Whites the experiences shared may not fully represent the experiences and perspectives of other races. However, because of our careful study of the history of interracial relations involving Caucasians with Native Americans, Latin Americans and Asian Americans we believe many of the underlying issues developed here do apply to other racial groups. Although, there are clear differences, we find many parallels in these histories. Therefore, members of all racial groups should find the content here relevant and useful.

We also acknowledge that an all-male set of contributors does not capture the difference in perspectives that a mixed-gender team might generate. The composition of our group was not consciously designed, but rather, it evolved organically among individuals who happened to be all men. We fully intend to add female voices to our work as it develops in the future.

It is our belief that the ultimate answer to race-related problems in our society does not lie in government programs or even in the laws of the land, although both are important in their own right. Rather, we believe the change needed must emanate from positive, personal action by individuals. To that end, we hope this book will facilitate your journey to a place of deeper understanding and more proactive behavior toward positively impacting race relations in our society.

HOW TO USE THIS BOOK

Each chapter has five components:

1. A principle and an associated action step that express how to promote positive race relations. In all, we will guide readers through twelve principles and related actions that empower them to be agents for positive change in the effort to build interracial harmony.

2. A story (or stories) that share the firsthand experiences of one or more group members and illustrate the principle and action step.

3. A set of questions to guide discussion and further learning about the issue(s) raised by the principle, action, and related stories. The questions for reflection, discussion, and further learning at the end of each chapter are particularly important in the process. We encourage readers to think deeply about each question and to respond in the spaces provided as they go along.

4. An author commentary that explains what the author wants the reader to derive from the story.

5. A declaration of commitment to follow the principle and execute the action step and a place to list an (optional) accountability partner to help you through the process.

The book is designed to be a guide for personal learning and growth as well as a tool to promote learning and discussion in groups. If readers choose to use the book to facilitate a group discussion, we suggest you observe the following guidelines:

1. Avoid dictating right and wrong responses or reactions to the issues raised.

2. Allow for different insights from the same action step and related story.

3. Promote respect for different viewpoints.

4. Encourage and facilitate participation in the discussion by members of the group who have less assertive communication styles.
5. Use the author commentaries to help frame potential lessons learned and insights gained from the chapter.
6. Handle disagreements that may arise without hostility and personal attacks.
7. Establish a consensus on the confidentiality of what group members share, such as agreeing nothing will be told to nonmembers with names of the person attached.
8. Explain that the statements of commitment to follow the steps are strongly encouraged but optional.

PRINCIPLE 1

Know Your Baseline

> **Step 1:** Take an inventory of the knowledge, attitudes, assumptions, and biases you have regarding interracial issues.

Story: "A Bias I Didn't Know I Had"

BY RICK WARREN

One Sunday, I was working at the café at our church with a young African American man whom I had come to know and really like through many Sundays of volunteering together. That day, he said, "Rick, here comes my wife and kids. I'd like to introduce you." When his wife, a pretty, Caucasian woman, walked up, the question popped into my head, "Why did she marry him?"

Thinking about this interaction as I walked to my car, I thought, "Are you kidding me, Rick? This is a Godly man. He has the character of someone you would hope your daughters would marry someday." It was then that I realized I had racial biases.

Questions and Steps for Reflection, Discussion, and Further Learning

1. Initiate a conversation with a person of another race about racial issues, and journal what you learn.
2. Make a list of the assumptions, beliefs, or perceptions you have about people of the _____ race.

_____

_____

_____

_____

3. What is your attitude toward interracial marriage? If not favorable, why not?

_____

_____

_____

_____

4. The story deals with a White person's reaction to a White woman's marriage to an African American man. Do African Americans (and members of other racial groups) also have adverse reactions to interracial marriage? If so, are the reasons the same?

_____

_____

_____

_____

Author Commentary

Very few people are overtly racially prejudiced against other people based on their race. What is also true is that racial prejudice or bias takes many forms and most of us are prejudiced on some level. In my case if you asked me before this incident happened if I had racial prejudices, I would have said, "absolutely not." I may have even mentioned that I have a number of African American friends. Yet, there is no question that my reason for questioning their match was based on the race of the racial minority party. This is a clear form of racial bias.

I challenge readers to do a careful and candid self-examination based on Step 1 and to candidly work through the questions and steps listed above for further learning. What you learn will be a good start toward achieving a higher level of personal competence on race and to becoming a part of the solution to racial problems in our nation.

Declaration of Intent

I will take an honest inventory of my knowledge, attitudes, assumptions, and biases related to interracial issues.

_____

Print your name here

_____ Date _____

Sign your name here

Accountability Partner (optional)

I commit that I will share my declaration with _____
and ask him/her to hold me accountable for acting on this declaration.

PRINCIPLE 2

Accept Discomfort

Step 2: Assess your willingness to be uncomfortable while you grow to become more competent in dealing with racial issues. Make a conscious decision to accept the discomfort that comes with personal development on this subject.

Story 1: "At the Bus Stop"

BY JAMES ROSE

The racial divide at Catholic Central High School was never more apparent than at the end of the school day. While the physical, daily transportation-based process we experienced occurred pragmatically, the starkness of it made me rife with anger. My anger was not toward the school or my classmates but toward society and the racial divide it imprinted on me every day.

When the final bell rang at the end of each school day, the young men of Catholic Central would go to their lockers and get their books, and then a social and physical migration would occur. The young White men would go out the rear or South exits of the building toward yellow school buses located at the rotunda at the back of the school or cross the back athletic fields to get to public buses that headed toward the western suburbs. The young African American men, on the other hand, would head out of the North exit at the front of the school to get on the public buses going east, into the interior of the city of Detroit. Rain or shine, hot or cold, the bell would ring, and we would go our separate ways.

Throughout my life, and particularly in the last decade, I have often been asked to share a time in my life when I experienced unconscious bias. Often, this was asked by a well-trained, White "diversity expert" in a mostly White diversity class that was sponsored by a predominantly White company. They often frame the question like this: "Please, take a moment and give honest consideration to a time in your life when you experienced unconscious bias. That is, if you can. If it is not too painful." The voice of the speaker stretches so far to convey empathy that it often seems insincere. I won't get into it more deeply here, but it is interesting to listen to attendees' stories. To avoid shocking the people attending the class with some of the more sordid tales in my struggle with race in America, I choose to tell my "At the Bus Stop" story for their listening and your reading.

As I said, every day the White boys at Catholic Central went West and the Black boys went East. One day, while all of us fellas were standing at our bus stop this young, White freshman boy came out to hang with the "brothers." We will call him Ken. I have no idea what made Ken choose to spend time with African American guys, but he did. I recall he was small and not very athletic but a nice guy. We spoke with him kindly and engaged with him in the light banter about sports, school, and girls that all boys our age discussed. Our conversation ended with everyone getting on the bus headed toward home in Detroit, while Ken stood at the bus stop and waved. He came a few times a week. Each time, we received him with interest and kindness as we were trained to be good to people, *all people*, and we took that lesson seriously as a group. We shared the underlying belief that if even one of us didn't treat everyone well, the result would be bad for all of us.

It was another ordinary day at the bus stop when Ken came out to hang out and check-in with the people. On this day, however, a guy of our group named Allen was not there. He was a ball player who was popular with the girls and his bus riding days had ended. Ken didn't know this and innocently asked, "Hey, where is Allen?"

I responded, "How should I know?"

Without the slightest hesitation, Ken said, "Well shouldn't you all know? Don't you all live together?"

We all broke out laughing at the same time. It was funny! And like Black friends often do, we took off on his statement with increasingly lude comments, like "Yea, you and Tommy share the same bedroom!" There was laughter, references to peoples' family members culminating with the inevitable mention of "your momma," and a never-ending barrage of related jokes and put-downs. If the jokes had been heard by or reported to our parents, we surely would have been put on punishment for a long time.

Ken quickly realized how illogical his assumption was and laughed with us. We took his question, "Don't you all live together" as an innocent error. Likewise, he saw no harm or wrong in our responses.

When the laughter settled down and we boarded our bus, I found myself wondering what other unspoken assumptions the White boys might be making about me and my "brothers." Perhaps, I thought, there were biases we wouldn't be able to shrug off with boyhood humor.

Questions for Reflection, Discussion, and Further Learning

1. Think of a time when you put yourself at risk or accepted discomfort to promote positive interracial relations. What was the outcome?

   _____

   _____

   _____

   _____

2. Why were the Black students in this case willing to laugh at the White student's mistake and continue accepting him as part of the group? What lessons about positive race relations can we learn from this?

   _____

   _____

   _____

   _____

3. At the end of the story, the author wonders what other assumptions (stereotypes and prejudices) the White students had about African Americans. What are some possible answers to his question? How can false assumptions be uncovered and eliminated?

_____

_____

_____

_____

Author Commentary:

Four things I hope readers will take from this story are:

- Never take your or another person's mistake about race too seriously. Sometimes people are just unaware.
- Have a sense of humor. Allow people who say or do something wrong an opportunity to laugh with you.
- Know that others are making assumptions about you, just as you are making assumptions about them. Gently correct those in the wrong and remember, people usually don't intend to discriminate or misjudge.
- A willingness to go out of one's comfort zone, as Ken was in the story, can lead to the formation of interracial associations that would not otherwise happen.

Story 2: "A White Guy in the Hood"
BY NICO MEYLAN

It did not take long after my wife and I began running a ministry in Detroit for me to realize that residential segregation was alive and well because the city and suburbs were divided by color. As I look back now, I realize we were naive to the reality of what was happening in our city and our country. Let me explain:

We moved into our mostly Black neighborhood because, based on the state of our nation, we believed we needed to be part of the solution and help create a bridge between Whites and Blacks. Another big part of our move was due to our relationship with God and believing He called us to both minister and live in the inner city.

Still, coming into our neighborhood was extremely uncomfortable. At first, nearly everyone on our street thought we were operating a drug house because, they thought, a young White couple living there must be related to drugs. Realizing this, some of our staff and I went to each house and introduced ourselves. This was extremely awkward.

Three weeks later, as I was driving back to my house, the police pulled me over in the front of my home not because we had broken the law but because the police profiled us as drug dealers. The officer was honest about his reason, saying, "Hey, you're White in a neighborhood where the majority of people living here are Black, and based on what we know, you have no business here." Some readers may be familiar with the charge of DWB, or Driving While Black, where some police officers stop Black motorists without proper cause. Here we had a new charge, DWW.

One of the programs we run involves playing basketball with and serving meals to people in our neighborhood. After a few months of having fun with our new friends and hanging out with our community, we started talking with them about what is happening in the United States regarding racism, the police, and relations between Whites and Blacks. We found out we were the only White friends they had. As we asked more questions, we also learned our neighbors had almost no relationship at all with people from different races.

Let me share a story about my neighbor friend John, who is African American. One day while hanging out, John and I started talking about relationships, specifically about our friendship. After a long time, he told me something I believe became the backbone of our relationship.

He said, "Nico, the first time I met you, we were talking about basketball. But then, you mentioned that you and your wife were okay financially but that you didn't have the money to go watch the (Detroit) Pistons play. I don't know if you know this, but for me it was the first time that a White guy spoke with this kind of humility, honesty, and realness about what his life was like."

At that moment, something clicked in me. I realized John thought White males had it all together. It didn't occur to him that we might face some of the same challenges he faced. But when we opened up and spoke candidly, John realized I wasn't that different from him and that we could relate.

I remember his reaction when we talked about tickets for the Piston's game. He seemed uncomfortable and walked away from me, which made me uncomfortable because I thought I had somehow offended him. I thought I failed in my relationship with him.

Rather than failing, though, my honesty helped build trust. Now we have a great friendship! We have our differences, but we embrace them because that's what friends do.

Questions and Steps for Reflection, Discussion, and Further Learning

1. In Story 2, the author's African American neighbor appears to have believed that all White people have it all together and did not face many financial worries. What other stereotypes do you think many African Americans have about Whites?

   _____

   _____

   _____

   _____

2. It is sometimes argued, and is the position of the authors of this book, that racial differences are not just physical but include differences of culture. Considering this, what is the difference between stereotyping and recognizing cultural differences among races?

   _____

   _____

   _____

   _____

3. The author of Story 2 accepted the discomfort of being one of only a few Whites in an African American neighborhood. How did he and his neighbors appear to have benefited from his willingness to endure this discomfort?

_____

_____

_____

_____

4. Story 2 deals in part with residential segregation. Many U.S. cities, including Detroit, have a sordid history of racial discrimination in access to housing. How does this history, and its effects, impact contemporary race relations/issues?

_____

_____

_____

_____

Author Commentary

I strongly believe the first bridge to seeing people coming together across racial lines is to learn how to be intentional with people of other races. We hide behind facades and stereotypes that create misunderstandings of who we truly are. When I first moved into my neighborhood, I felt uncomfortable and didn't have a plan to befriend my neighbors. But I did become a friend because I was myself. I was transparent and willing to be uncomfortable to pursue relationships with them. We must realize there will be some level of discomfort when we first meet someone who is racially or culturally different than we are or when we are in situations where there are few people of our own racial identity present. However, we must learn to push through that discomfort and find common interests. By doing so, we will build real bridges with other races and cultural groups.

Declaration of Intent

I make a conscious decision to accept being uncomfortable so I may grow and develop as a supporter of positive race relations.

_____
Print your name here

_____ Date _____
Sign your name here

Accountability Partner (optional)

I commit that I will share my declaration with _____
and ask him/her to hold me accountable for acting on this declaration.

PRINCIPLE 3

Understand the Personal Impact of Race

Step 3: Answer the question: How has my race affected my life experiences?

Story 1: "The Racial Integration of My School"
BY DEXTER JAMES

When I was fifteen years old, I attended St. Joe High, a Catholic school in downtown Atlanta, Georgia. That year, my school closed and my class merged with the students at St. Pius X, an all-White Catholic school in suburban Chamblee. On the first day of class, I witnessed the frustration of White parents when they saw Black students standing in front of the school. I could see disappointment in their faces as they drove off with their children because they refused to accept Black Catholic children in "their" White Catholic school. Over the next days, about 25 percent of the White families took their children out of the school.

Questions/Steps for Reflection, Discussion, and Further Learning

1. Members of the majority, or dominant, race group often do not see how their race affects their life experiences. For many, race only affects members of racial minority groups. By contrast, most racial minorities are fully aware that being White in our culture grants benefits in virtually every important sphere of life. The question posed in Step 3 is especially

important for Whites to reflect on and understand. Regardless of your race, write one or two ways in which you believe your race has affected your life.

_____

_____

_____

_____

_____

2. The term "White privilege" is sometimes used to describe how race affects Whites in U.S. culture. How do you react (e.g. anger, confusion, defense, affirmation) when you hear this term? Is it possible and appropriate to acknowledge White privilege while at the same time recognizing that White people have their own struggles and obstacles to achievement? How can we express the role of race in a way that recognizes that both are true? Write a statement that expresses this balance of perspectives for you.

_____

_____

_____

_____

3. When some racial minorities respond to the question posed in Step 3, they imply the negative effects of racial bias are the cause of nearly all their troubles. Is this realistic? Why or why not?

_____

_____

_____

_____

What problems does such a mindset potentially create for those minorities who hold it ?

_____

_____

_____

_____

4. Some racial minorities, and even some White people, say minorities cannot be racists? Is that true ? Why or why not ?

_____

_____

_____

_____

Author Commentary

As a Black man in America, I learned from this early experience with prejudice that although we are in a fight for racial justice we must be willing to forgive and not become bitter. For a time, this and related experiences caused me to be somewhat resentful toward White people. I even fought with a White kid over a school test. Some of that resentment carried over into my adult life, making it harder for me to trust White people. As time went on however, my development as a Christian who was learning of the ways of Christ paired with meeting and getting to know many good and caring White people allowed me to overcome these earlier hurts and attitudes.

Resources for Further Learning

- "Overcoming White Blindness" by Chris Williamson – <u>Chriswilliamson.home.blog</u>

Story 2: "A Very Scary Day at High School"

BY TAYLOR COX JR.

High school for me was a challenging time. Just before my first year started, my mother unexpectedly passed away at the age of 35. With the support of my dad and my grandmother, my sisters and I carried on as best we could. I was a good student. During my last two years my weekdays consisted of classes from 8-12, a half-hour lunch break, and work from 12:30-4:30 as a file clerk at Reliance Insurance Company in Detroit. After that, I did homework, watched an hour of television, and then went to bed.

One day, while I was sitting in study hall, two police officers entered and spoke to my high school counselor. When they came out of her office they came straight to my desk. They told me that I had to come with them. I asked why. They did not answer. Instead, they took me from the room, put me into a police car, and drove me downtown to Detroit Police Headquarters.

I continued to ask what it was all about but received no reply. Once at the police station, I asked if could make a phone call but was told I could do so later. After what seemed like a long time, I was placed in a line up with several other people and told how to stand and where to look. There, I thought about how easily I could be misidentified and held as a criminal awaiting trial. I knew how difficult it would have been for my dad to raise bail money. No one in my family knew where I was or what was happening to me. I was, in a word, traumatized.

When the lineup ended, officers took me to a room where I was told I was suspected of having committed a crime, but the victim had not identified me as the guilty person. I asked on what basis I was suspected and was told that a young woman had been raped near a veterinary clinic on Livernois Avenue. They said I was suspected because I was a Black person and was in the file as someone who had taken my dog to that clinic. I was then taken back to the school and let out of the car. I was fully aware of how close I had come to a life behind bars.

Questions for Reflection, Discussion, and Further Learning:

1. Do you believe the legal and court systems in the U.S. provide equal justice to all people regardless of race or socio-economic status? If not, how do you believe race and socioeconomics affect justice in our legal system?

   _____

   _____

   _____

   _____

2. What could we do to make our legal systems more just? What could you personally do? What can police departments do? What legislation would help, etc.?

   _____

   _____

   _____

   _____

   _____

3. Recent events in the U.S. have spotlighted the experiences young African Americans have with police. In some cases, these encounters resulted in the death of the racial minority stopped by police. How do racial stereotypes and prejudices held by both parties influence these situations?

   _____

   _____

   _____

   _____

4. What steps can be taken to minimize these deadly confrontations?

_____

_____

_____

_____

5. In Story 2, what specific police actions, if any, do you believe were unjust or should have been done differently?

_____

_____

_____

_____

Author Commentary:

In our criminal justice system, there are many ways in which race and socio-economic status affect the process. For example, the ability to afford good lawyers and bail often determines levels of justice. The race of the suspect affects the likelihood of being stopped, arrested, found guilty, and of receiving a stiff sentence. Some research indicates that sentencing is more harsh if the victim is White.

It is also true that the behavior of the people that police stop is an important contributor to outcomes. In my case, I have always been careful to be courteous to law enforcement officers and this has served me well. Similarly, expecting harsh treatment from police can lead racial minorities to behave in a manner that creates a self-fulfilling prophecy. In other words, the officers become hostile in response to hostility from the suspect. Change must occur on both sides for real progress to be made.

Story 3: "A Lesson in Intra-race Racial Dynamics"
BY TERRY OPREA

As a Caucasian man who owned a marketing and communications firm, I learned from an African American friend how painful intra-race prejudice can be. Both educational and professional experience are at the root of this kind of discrimination.

I live in Metropolitan Detroit, which has been rapidly reviving after decades of decline. In many ways, there is still serious segregation between the haves and the have-nots in the area, with extreme poverty mostly clustered in the predominantly African American city of Detroit.

Julia (not her real name), who is African American, was an executive for a major national corporation. She was transferred to the Detroit regional offices from the west coast. One of her jobs as a vice president involved running public affairs in the area. Julia embraced her new position with enthusiasm, networking with community-based organizations, nonprofit agencies, and community leaders to be a great corporate citizen representing her firm. I got to know her well during that process. What a great heart she had for the underserved people in the city!

About a year after Julia arrived, she decided she wanted to become personally involved as a volunteer by helping alleviate Detroit's historically high levels of functional illiteracy. At the time, illiteracy in the city was approaching 50 percent. Julia began volunteering as a tutor to teens and young adults.

In one of her early assignments, a teenager she was tutoring told Julia, "You're not Black."

"What are you talking about," a stunned Julia said.

Her student became more specific. The conversation can be summed up as: "You're well educated, well-read, well-dressed, have a good job and make good money, so you're not really Black."

At first, Julia wrote it off to poor behavior from one isolated individual. But she was wrong. As she continued in her work, it happened repeatedly. Baffled by it all, Julia shared with me how deeply distressed and hurt she was and how the encounters began to affect her confidence about interacting with the community. Essentially, she said, "I'm giving of myself, my time, and my energy to help the underserved in my community—people of my own race. My help is not only being rejected but my own education and professional success is being interpreted as a sign that I'm a poser and not really of my race."

After a few years, Julia had enough and transferred back to her home city in California, where she lives today.

Questions for Reflection, Discussion, and Further Learning

1. Have you ever encountered or been told about an experience like that described in Julia's story? If so, briefly describe it here.

   _____

   _____

   _____

   _____

2. Why would the teen in the story relate characteristics, such as education, dress, and job, to Julia's race?

   _____

   _____

   _____

   _____

3. Many African Americans say one must be bi-cultural to successfully navigate in both White and Black settings. How could this idea help us understand what is happening in this story?

   _____

_____

_____

_____

4. What does this story tell us about the extent to which the United States is a racialized society (i.e. a society where race has wide ranging effects)?

_____

_____

_____

_____

_____

Author Commentary:

I had not previously heard of the kind of intra-racial prejudice Julia revealed. On reflection, I realize the root of it is socio-economic classism taken to an extreme. The collapse of the public education system in Detroit created generations of kids and young adults who saw themselves wholly separated from educational and professional success. Poverty creates an additional gulf between older middle and upper-income African Americans and kids and young adults from lower-income households.

As I thought about this more, I realized I'm guilty of the same thing—in reverse. In the Caucasian community, how many times have I thought condescendingly about so-called trailer trash and rednecks? How many times have I judged my neighbors based on their cars, houses, or even lawns? How many times have I interpreted dialect as a sign of ignorance among those of my own race?

"Love your neighbor as yourself" is an ancient directive that rings true even today. I have resolved to keep that dictum front-of-mind.

Story 4: "Race and Violence"

BY DEXTER JAMES

I was about six years old and living in Atlanta when I had an experience I have never forgotten. One Spring day, at about three o'clock in the afternoon, I was walking down the street with other children when my grandmother and several older men and women from my neighborhood suddenly came up the street yelling something. When they got close enough, I could hear them saying, "Run! Run! Get to the house fast!"

At home, I looked out the window and saw why we were told to run. Carloads of Ku Klux Klan members wearing their white robes were driving down our street—some of them standing on the running boards of their cars. I didn't fully understand then what was going on, but I soon learned the men were patrolling our neighborhood in hopes of intimidating and violently attacking any Black people who might be on the streets.

Questions for Reflection, Discussion, and Further Learning

1. The incident described in Story 4 was a familiar one in the South in the early and mid- 1900s. However, the attitudes that prompted Klan members to act violently then toward members of their own community because they were a different race still exist. We see this in many contemporary incidents where violence, including murder, occurs because of someone's race. What thoughts and emotions are stirred for you when you hear of an incident like the one in the story?

_____

_____

_____

_____

_____

2. How might an experience like this affect the author's future relationships with White people?

_____

_____

_____

_____

3. Most Americans living today have never personally experienced racially motivated violence. Does this mean they are not affected by violent race-based incidents that happen to other people of their race? Why or why not?

_____

_____

_____

_____

4. How might Black people who are not directly involved in incidents where police use excessive force in encounters with African Americans be affected by such incidents?

_____

_____

_____

_____

_____

5. Some people say too much is made of the George Floyd and Breonna Taylor incidents —where African Americans were unjustly killed by police—because most violence against Black people is committed by other Blacks. Do you agree with this thinking? If not, how should we respond to this argument?

_____

_____

_____

Author Commentary

After I came to understand what was happening, I remember wondering why Black people wouldn't stand up to those men. It was only later that I came to understand that Blacks had little to no protection or support from law enforcement and thus would only have compounded their trouble if they aggressively stood up to the Klan and similar bigoted groups. It did, however, make me more determined to be strong and stand up for myself.

Declaration of Intent

I recognize that my race has had a significant effect on my life experiences and will become more aware of how race affects my life experiences and those of others. I will also strive to avoid assuming race is the cause of my life experiences when the actual cause is something different.

_____

Print your name here

_____ Date _____

Sign your name here

Accountability Partner (optional)

I commit that I will share my declaration with _____
and ask him/her to hold me accountable for acting on this declaration.

PRINCIPLE 4

Become an Active Listener

Step 4: Initiate and capitalize on opportunities to hear, and actively listen to, the stories and perspectives of associates of other race groups.

Story: "Listening on the Flight Home"

BY DAVID THOMAS

Back in 1995, I was on a plane heading out on a business trip when a young African American woman was seated next to me. We began talking, and I learned her father was a minister who pastored a church in Chicago and that she was serious about her Christian faith. She was pleasant and transparent, and we struck up a good conversation about religion, philosophy, politics, etc.

At that time, I was supporting conservative Robert Dole for president while she was supporting Bill Clinton. Because of her faith, I felt certain that character would be a high priority for her in a candidate. Since I believed Bill Clinton was less principled than Robert Dole, I asked her why she was supporting Clinton. The message from Bob Dole at that time was "Let's bring back the good old days."

Her answer caused me to understand her preference. She clearly articulated that "back in the good old days, I couldn't live where I wanted to live, couldn't get a job where I wanted to work, and, in many places, I couldn't eat where I wanted to eat. I couldn't go to the school I wanted to or even sit on the bus where I wanted to sit."

None of this had occurred to me though I did not view myself as being bigoted or prejudiced in any way. However, I am not African American and that difference explains a lot about why I never thought of the "good old days" in those terms. Listening to her broadened my perspective and made me aware of blind spots I did not realize I had.

Questions and Steps for Reflection, Discussion, and Further Learning

1. How often in the last 12 months have you had a conversation with someone of another race in which he/she shared about life experiences particularly dealing with race?

   _____

   _____

   _____

   _____

2. Are you a good listener? Do other people say that you are? If not, what steps will you take to become a better listener?

   _____

   _____

   _____

   _____

3. Are you able to listen, hear, and understand what other people are saying before drawing conclusions or making judgments?

   _____

   _____

   _____

   _____

4. At the time of this writing, there is a controversy in the political realm like the one mentioned in the above story. President Donald Trump campaigned on the slogan "Make America Great Again." Discuss the

different, racially correlated connotations associated with this slogan with a mixed-race group of people or with a person of a different race than you. As you do so, be sure to practice good listening skills. Record your thoughts and insights gained here.

_____

_____

_____

_____

Author Commentary

I would like readers to consider the following insights and ideas related to my story.

1. Listening allows us to see things from different perspectives. We should not feel threatened by these differences.
2. Use listening skills and transparency to overcome the fear of others.
3. Do not let differences of perspective stop you from listening for understanding.
4. When we know someone, we are less likely to want to hurt them.

Declaration of Intent

I will actively seek out and listen to the stories and perspectives of associates of other race groups.

_____

Print your name here

_____ Date _____

Sign your name here

Accountability Partner (optional)

I commit that I will share my declaration with _____
and ask him/her to hold me accountable for acting on this declaration.

5

PRINCIPLE 5

Address the Power Dynamics of Race

Step 5: Examine race-related power dynamics in the groups and organizations in which you have membership and work to create an appropriate distribution of access to power among race groups.

Story: "Power Dynamics of U.S. Race Relations"

BY TAYLOR COX JR.

For many years as a consultant on workplace diversity, I observed a common pattern when viewing racial demographic profiles. The information below is from actual profiles taken from real organizations.

Organization 1

- Percent of racial minorities on payroll = 10 %
- Percent of racial minorities in twenty-one management jobs = 0 %

Organization 2

- Percent of racial minorities on payroll = 15 %
- Percent of racial minorities in senior management jobs = 0 %

Organization 3

Percent of college-degreed people in professional jobs with 14 years or more of service who have reached upper-management positions:

- Whites = 55 %
- Racial-minority men = 16 %
- Racial-minority women = 0

These examples reveal a consistent pattern of authority distribution by race group: Racial minorities (defined as African Americans, Latin Americans, Asian Americans and Native Americans) are typically, and often drastically, underrepresented in the power structure of organizations.

Although authority is not the only source of power, it is arguably the most important. This pattern of authority distribution is often observed beyond the business arena as well. For example, roughly 75 percent of National Football League players are racial minorities, mostly African American. Yet, only about 25 percent of head coaches and 13 percent of general managers are racial minorities.

As we think about how race impacts life in America and how we can help stop racial division and promote positive race relations, it behooves us to give careful attention to the power dynamics of racial diversity.

Questions for Reflection, Discussion, and Further Learning

1. What are the reasons for the pattern of authority distribution by race as shown in the above story?

   _____

   _____

   _____

2. What are the implications or effects of differential access to positions of authority for people of different racial groups?

   _____

   _____

   _____

   _____

3. Teachers occupy important positions of power, affecting the lives of people in their formative years. With that in mind, what has been the racial composition of the teaching faculty in the schools you have attended?

_____

_____

_____

_____

4. How might the racial composition of teachers in your life have affected your educational and post-education views and experiences?

_____

_____

_____

_____

5. What can or should be done to promote a more proportional distribution of racial groups in authority structures (i.e. reduce the gap between overall membership and membership in leadership positions for racial minorities)?

_____

_____

_____

_____

6. What can you do to change the power distribution of racial groups in organizations where you have membership?

_____

_____

Author Commentary

The pattern of distribution of authority shown in this story is a common one, and it has many implications. They include effects on income and the ability to build wealth, differential ability to influence group and organizational decisions, policy and culture, and effects on personal confidence and self-esteem. The reasons for the lower participation of racial minorities in positions of authority vary. In some cases, differences of education, experience, seniority, and other factors that qualify people to lead is a major reason. In such cases, we must assess whether race is impacting access to these qualifications. Here one will find many instances of race impact, which if addressed, will produce a more racially balanced distribution of power.

In other cases, direct race-related bias is operating. For example, one of the realities of human behavior is that when qualifications are equal or nearly equal, most people favor those of their own race when making decisions about advancing people to positions of influence. Because White people have historically dominated decision-making positions in the U.S., this reality has naturally led to the preservation of White domination in positions of authority.

As the reader grapples with these issues, the reflection and discussion will allow for insight into additional aspects of race relations. For example, what are the implications of going through twelve years of primary education and perhaps even college and never having a teacher who is a racial minority? And how does the fact that White people have, on average, almost ten times the net worth of African Americans impact the power dynamics of race? These and other questions will provide a rich time of self-reflection and dialogue.

Declaration of Intent

I am committed to examining the relative access to authority and other sources of power between race groups in the groups and organizations in which I am a member and to do my part to promote racial equality in access to power consistent with individual qualifications.

_____

Print name here

_____ Date _____

Sign name here

Accountability Partner (optional)

I commit that I will share my declaration with _____
and ask him/her to hold me accountable for acting on this declaration.

PRINCIPLE 6

Invest in Personal Education

> **Step 6:** Invest in multiple forms of on-going personal education about racial dynamics.

Story: "Another Day at the Office..."

BY JIM ROSE

A colleague angrily asked, "What do you expect us to do, fire all the White people and hire Blacks in their place?"

"No," I replied. "Just give fair consideration and opportunities for more Blacks to be hired into the company."

After another majority-race person in the room retorted, "What exactly do you mean? Be specific," I chose to remain silent for the duration of my company's first session on diversity and inclusion. The frustration and anger in the response to my comments let me know I struck a chord. The hypocrisy of having a policy to promote diversity with no corresponding action was thoroughly exposed. Managers would either be accountable for acting on corporate diversity policies or resume doing nothing about the extraordinary lack of racial diversity within the organization. I had done the best I could do. I had said my piece. I pushed the conversation to the edge and knew it was time to be silent and let the red-faced anger cool down.

When the professional facilitator said, "Folks, I think we should take a break now," everyone but me and the facilitator left the room. Then she asked if I was OK.

"I am fine," I said. "I have been Black all my life, and hearing how they have acted in private all these years doesn't affect me."

"But are you okay?" she asked.

"I am fine," I said, finishing the exchange. I am not sure I was fine, but I certainly was familiar with the adrenaline flush under my tongue. It was a feeling I had when I repressed my anger at what seemed to me to be the blatant naivety of Whites who seemed not to recognize even the simplest manifestations of bias that have punished and tortured me every day of my life.

After the heated exchange, I made sure I stayed focused and let the guys in the room know I was still a member of the team and that when this was over, we would return to working together on the mission of the company. It was surprising how quickly attitudes were reset. By the end of the session, they were back to their chipper selves. The lite banter, chiding, and joking returned as though nothing had happened—as though I had not challenged systemic biases and, what I perceived to be, racist behaviors within the company.

The racial-majority individuals present knew they could and would return to their chipper banter, chipper jobs, chipper families, and chipper lives. And I knew I would return to the same place I was before joining the meeting room—back to my not-so chipper life amongst them suffering in silence another day at the office.

Several days later, Al, a White colleague, came to my office and asked if I had a minute. When I invited him in, he gently closed the door behind him and found a seat.

"Listen," Al said, "The comments you made at the diversity-and-inclusion session were spot on. You told the facts and spoke the truth about your situation here at the company. Tough to listen to, but I believe everything you said was your experience. I would like to learn more about what it is like for Blacks to work at this company and in corporate America in general. Could you recommend any books I might read on the subject?"

I was stunned. Al, who had attended our session on diversity and inclusion, was someone I considered the very definition of "chipper." But I also knew Al was a good man, always a gentleman, 100 percent serious, and a businessman through and through.

When I got past my surprise, I said, "I know of a book that will provide you plenty of insights into the issue of being Black in corporate America. Pick up a copy of 'The Rage of a Privileged Class' by Ellis Cose." When he asked where to purchase the book, I decided to test his seriousness and directed him to a Black-owned bookstore in a neighborhood that I was reluctant to enter. Al, being specific and purposeful as always, stood up, shook my hand, thanked me, and left my office.

I appreciated Al's inquiry; no one in my lifetime had ever taken this step with me. I then quickly reached out to some African American friends and colleagues and asked them if any of them had ever been asked about being African American in corporate America. They all said no.

I didn't expect Al to get the book; even if he did, I certainly didn't expect him to read it. In fact, I felt sure he would never engage me on the subject again. I figured once the discomfort of the meeting had subsided, Al, like everyone else of his pedigree would simply return to his chipper life.

I was wrong! Al called a short time later asking if I would come to his office. I honestly thought he wanted to have a discussion on a completely different business-related subject. When I arrived, Al, who wore formal corporate attire with suit and tie, motioned for us to sit at his round table. Then he produced a copy of Ellis Cose's "The Rage of a Privileged Class."

It wasn't a fresh, unbroken, unread copy; the book's pages were turned down. It had notes in the margins, highlighted passages, and note cards in the back. He had *read* this book.

With typical enthusiasm, Al said, "I read the book you recommended thoroughly, and I have some questions."

For the next hour, we had the most engaging and honest conversation I ever had about race in corporate America. Al had taken the time to become knowledgeable about the subject and had shown he was truly curious about the issues.

By the end of the meeting, he had demonstrated that he was more empathetic toward me and other African Americans in the company. He said: "This entire experience has changed me. Your comments during the session were difficult to hear, but I trusted you were telling the truth from your perspective. Also, the book was difficult to read but it has enlightened me, and I will be different as a result," Al said this in pristine business language and with a demeanor that indicated he was flat out serious. Subsequently, Al became a pragmatic champion of diversity and inclusion in that company, which is something that, to this day, I appreciate and respect.

Questions for Reflection, Discussion, and Further Learning

1. What reactions did you have to this story? What stands out to you?

   _____

   _____

   _____

   _____

2. Many organizations are engaging in this type of facilitated discussion of race and other forms of social identity differences. What does the story indicate about the likely costs and benefits of this kind of educational activity?

   _____

   _____

   _____

   _____

   _____

3. What steps can be taken to maximize the benefits and minimize the costs of "diversity training?"

_____

_____

_____

_____

4. What specific actions by the author and his associate, Al, were important to bringing about the positive outcomes reported in the story?

_____

_____

_____

_____

5. The author states that he had never experienced a person seeking him out to talk about racial issues the way Al did. Why is this kind of engagement between people rare?

_____

_____

_____

_____

6. Al's follow up to get the book, read it, and then initiate a discussion about it shows he was highly motivated to be more educated about racial issues. What return on his investment of time are he and his company likely to get?

_____

_____

_____

Author Commentary

Key learnings I hope readers get from this story are:

- Never underestimate how serious a person can become about race-related education based on a single experience.
- When in the heat of the discussion, remain focused on what is important: understanding.
- Behind a difficult conversation there is often an opportunity to build a lifetime friendship

Declaration of Intent

I will invest in multiple forms of on-going education about racial dynamics.

_____

Print name here

_____ Date _____

Sign name here

Accountability Partner (optional)

I commit that I will share my declaration with _____
and ask him/her to hold me accountable for acting on this declaration.

PRINCIPLE 7

Know Your History

Step 7: Develop and implement a specific plan of research and study on the history of race relations.

Story: "A Short Comment on the History of Race Relations in the U.S."
BY TAYLOR COX JR.

When I was attending public school in the 1950s and early '60s, very little was taught about the history of race relations in the United States. The types of books often used were like "A Short History of the United States" by John Spencer Bassett, which I still have in in my library. Here's an excerpt:

> "Slavery was a hard institution and the Negro, being unenlightened and submissive by nature, invited severe treatment to induce him to labor hard and refrain from evil conduct. Whipping was used freely because the masters felt it was the punishment most effective with him (page 470, Bassett)."

It was not until I reached college and had access to a course on African American history, taught by the only Black instructor at the university at that time, that I became more educated about the true history. In subsequent years, I gained considerable knowledge from reading the work of historians, such as John Hope Franklin, Lerone Bennett Jr., and Dee Brown. Like any true history, the history of race relations is fraught with complexity, contradictions, and scenarios that are subject to multiple interpretations. However, the unmistakable pattern in the history of Anglo American relations with African Americans, Latin Americans (especially of Mexican heritage), Native Americans, and Asian Americans from the 1600s until the mid-twentieth century includes various forms of exploitation and restriction of rights. Among the most crucial often overlooked or downplayed topics and events for readers to know in this area are:

- Slavery of Blacks of African descent from the early 1600s to 1865
- The Trail of Tears: the displacement of Native Americans from the Southeastern U.S. by President Andrew Jackson
- Land disenfranchisement of Native Americans during the 1800s
- Killing of Native Americans and taking of land from Mexican Americans during the California gold rush
- The Chinese Exclusion Act
- Jim Crow laws and related treatment of African Americans in the post-reconstruction period (1880s to the early1960s)
- The internment of Japanese Americans during World War II

This list is by no means complete, but it is a good sampling of things about which every American should be well educated. A knowledge of this history provides context and proper perspective for understanding contemporary race relations and dynamics. Although many people think of these events as ancient history, consider this: Harriet Tubman, who was born a slave and personally responsible for bringing 300 slaves to freedom on the underground railroad, was alive until 1913. She was therefore a contemporary of my grandparents. Moreover, I was in high school before the U.S. Civil Rights Act, which made racial discrimination officially illegal, became law.

Questions for Reflection, Discussion, and Further Learning

1. On a scale of 1 (uninformed) to 10 (very well-informed), how would you rate your knowledge of the history of race relations and race-related issues in the U.S.?

    African American and White relations/issues _____

    Native American and White relations/issues _____

    Latin American and White relations/issues _____

Asian American and White relations/issues _____

2. Do you believe it is important to know the history of race in the country? Why or why not?

_____

_____

_____

_____

3. An important historical influence on the way that different racial groups are perceived is how they have been portrayed in the media especially in film. With this in mind, what are your thoughts on how various racial groups have been portrayed in film since the 1920s.

_____

_____

_____

_____

4. What effect do you think these portrayals have had on race dynamics in the U.S.? (be specific)

_____

_____

_____

_____

Author Commentary

Although the teaching of the history of race relations has improved, most people will not get a comprehensive, truthful understanding of the history of race in the U.S. from the standard instruction provided in our primary and higher-education programs. There are even many racial minorities who are not truly knowledgeable about the history of race in the U.S. Therefore, most of us need to invest in such an education. Doing so will help dispel myths and distortions of history that media outlets, family oral histories, and the like have presented. It also helps us understand one another better.

I have spent much of my adult life researching, writing, and consulting about social identity issues, including racial dynamics, and still have much to learn. We learn a great deal about race relations, as discussed in other chapters of this book, from engaging people of different racial backgrounds in dialogues, friendships, and other positive interactions. However, more structured pursuits of learning such as reading and watching videos adds a great deal to our understanding and ability to be a positive force for change. My own educational journey has been interesting, thought-provoking, emotional, and enriching, and I believe yours will be the same.

Resources for Further Learning:

Books

- "From Slavery to Freedom" by John Hope Franklin
- "Before the Mayflower" by Lerone Bennett Jr.
- "Bury My Heart at Wounded Knee: An Indian History of the American West" by Dee Brown

Videos

- "The Chinese Exclusion Act," directed by Ric Burns and Li-Shin Yu
- "The West" (especially episodes 4 and 6), directed by Stephen Ives
- "Slavery and the Making of America," a PBS series

- "For Love of Liberty: The Story of America's Black Patriots," from Mill Creek Entertainment
- "Reconstruction: The Second Civil War," a PBS film

Declaration of Intent

I will develop and implement a specific plan to further educate myself on the history of interracial relations concerning the major racial groups of the United States (or of your home country).

_____

Print your name here

_____   _____

Sign your name   Date

Accountability Partner (optional)

I commit that I will share my declaration with _____
and ask him/her to hold me accountable for acting on this declaration.

PRINCIPLE 8

Get the Facts on Current Events

Step 8: Consistently read or listen to high-quality, factual material on current events related to race.

Story: "The Case of Statues of the Confederacy"

BY BRADLEY THOMAS

Many people in the White community take for granted the impact and underestimate the brutality of the Jim Crow era and civil rights struggles on the African American community. Some see life as being "fair" now and believe we should all just move on. I recently had a business acquaintance say his children never "saw race" until they learned of slavery and the Civil War in school, and from that, he said, they became jaded. This illustrates that, for some, education or attention to racial issues is a negative and not to be pursued.

I believe this is wrong thinking. We must live in truth and not revise history or ignore current events related to race in order to remain comfortable. Once we start ignoring the facts of past and current events, we lose perspective on the future.

An issue receiving public interest and headline news recently was the tearing down of monuments in the South that commemorated Confederate War heroes. This was met with great controversy. As recently as 2015 the Confederate flag, a symbol of the South's secession because of, among other things, the ability to maintain slavery, flew over the South Carolina State House. Many in the South still view these monuments with immense pride and cite them not as images of a pro-slavery war but rather as honoring important leaders in history. More recently, President Donald Trump referred to removing the statues as "foolish" and asked, "Who's next George Washington?"

While there is room for honest disagreement about whether these statues should be removed, it behooves us all to take a closer look at when and why they were erected in the first place. Were they, as many believe, constructed during or just after the Civil War to commemorate Southern pride? A close look suggests otherwise:

According to *Business Insider* and the Southern Poverty Law Center, the number of Confederate memorial installations peaked around 1910, fifty years after the end of the Civil War and at the height of Jim Crow—an era defined by segregation and disenfranchisement laws against Black Americans. Confederate installations spiked again in the 1950s and '60s, during the Civil Rights Movement. (See the chart below)

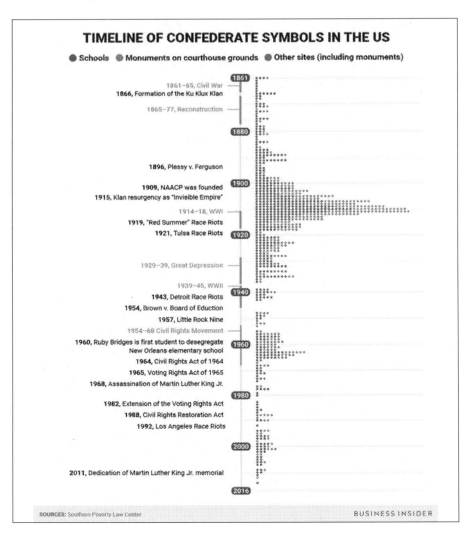

As you can see from the chart, most of the monuments were erected in direct correlation to the growing unrest among the White community with attempts at the integration and equalization of African Americans. It is our duty as good people who believe in equality to search out the truth in any argument. Resources are available and sources must be verified because behind every emotional argument is discoverable truth that leads to better interaction and more enlightened race relations.

Questions for Reflection, Discussion, and Further Learning

1. The story above deals with only one race-related issue that has been in the news recently. What current events related to race have you observed? To what extent have you investigated any of these to confirm information presented by the media?

   _____

   _____

   _____

2. What steps can we take as individuals to minimize the risk of drawing false conclusions from information the media presents?

   _____

   _____

   _____

3. Have you ever discovered that something you believed was quite different after doing research or talking to others? If so, describe that here?

   _____

   _____

   _____

   _____

4. How do you believe social media has impacted race relations in the U.S.? What steps can we take as individuals to help social media have a more positive impact on race relations?

_____

_____

_____

_____

Author Commentary

We need facts to acquire knowledge and continually grow in racial harmony. There are ample resources we can use to "fact check" our beliefs and what we hear from associates and the media. We must strive to build our knowledge so we can combat the untruths we hear and base our views and actions on valid information. Many media outlets provide half-truths and distortions; thus, we must be diligent in our quest to be accurately informed about current events that warrant attention and help inform our perspectives on race and other topics of importance.

Declaration of Intent

I will consistently read, listen to, and research high-quality, accurate information about current race-related events and not rely on news media reports as a sole source of information.

_____

Print your name here

_____ Date _____

Sign your name here

Accountability Partner (optional)

I commit that I will share my declaration with _____
and ask him/her to hold me accountable for acting on this declaration.

PRINCIPLE 9

Make Race Discussable

Step 9: Invite and initiate discussion about race in the groups and interpersonal relationships in which you participate.

Story: "Discussing Race at Work: Is your workplace a safe place for discussion of race-related issues?"

BY SHANNON GASTON

One reason progress toward dismantling centuries-old race-related problems has been slow is that many of those who have benefitted from the status quo deny racial bias or don't understand the magnitude to which race-related problems impact our collective quality of life. One way to look at the way race impacts our everyday lives is to examine our individual workplaces. Racial minorities often struggle to bring their whole selves into their workplaces for fear that such authenticity would be perceived as an unwelcome threat to the status quo. Unless we make race discussable in these places where we spend most of our lives, many racial minorities will continue to view the workplace as unsafe.

I was once hired by an organization with a racial demographic profile that did not accurately reflect the predominantly African American urban center it served. Ill-informed decisions which were consistently being made by its nearly all-White leadership hindered our effectiveness and our ability to achieve desired outcomes. An organization culture had set in that hemorrhaged talented people, and the racial diversity of the community being served was not leveraged to ensure racial diversity at the decision-making table.

As a new member of the team and an African American, I hoped my perspective, although often counter to the culture, might be sufficiently valued to be considered. I had been recruited to provide a valuable service that aligned with the organization's stated values and goals, but I knew that if I could not be my authentic self, my ability to contribute, and indeed my tenure with the organization, would be short.

After a year, I communicated my frustration with not being heard, candidly conveying my disappointments and explaining how racial issues were affecting my work and our organizational effectiveness. I did this for my mental well-being as well as to help the organization. I respectfully and frankly shared my specific experiences and concerns about the organization with top leadership, all of whom were White men. While I was prepared to lose my job the next day, I felt I would at least have peace and assurance that the organization had experienced the real me and that I would have a clear conscience because I graciously challenged them toward what I thought was a better path forward.

However, instead of being dismissed, what actually happened was that a series of deep, meaningful conversations ensued—first interpersonally and then among board and staff members. These conversations created opportunities for deeper relationships and sustained dialogue around solutions. Also, the organization made key staffing changes in the ensuing months.

If your workplace is like most and conversations about race are being avoided altogether or are perceived as being harmful and divisive, I urge you to take proactive steps to make race-related issues discussable. Progress may be slow, but the elephant in the room will become visible and staff of all races will be able to freely speak their truth.

Questions for Reflection, Discussion, and Further Learning

1. Is your workplace a safe place for people to speak honestly and openly about race-related issues? Why or why not?

_____

_____

_____

_____

_____

2. Think of an example of when an honest conversation about race took place at your workplace or in another organizational setting. Describe how it went. Did it affect any relational dynamics thereafter? If so, in what way?

_____

_____

_____

_____

3. Does your workplace have a formal or informal policy around potentially uncomfortable in-office conversations (i.e. discussing controversial subjects such as politics or race)? If so, what is the policy? Is it helpful or harmful in your view? What impact is it having on workplace relationships and effectiveness?

_____

_____

_____

_____

4. How does the ethnic composition of your workplace affect the existence or form of conversations about race-related issues?

_____

_____

_____

_____

5. Some say that by talking about a problem we make it bigger and more dangerous. Do you agree with this? Why or why not?

_____

_____

_____

_____

Author Commentary

I have seen the way the "angry Black male" stereotype is used to create a wedge that prevents honest cross-cultural dialogue. I have also seen examples in the Black community of why that caricature persists. In its worst manifestations, it's an unjustifiable rant that generalizes too much and stops short of solutions. I have also seen the way White fragility manifests and often hijacks conversations that involve race if they are not set up well. The issue of race in America is complex, painful, and sometimes overwhelming. In the West, we, especially men, are socialized to be rugged individualists who think logically and behave as "fixers."

None of these mindsets lend themselves well to understanding, empathy, and authentic cross-cultural relationship building. I believe that W.E.B. DuBois was correct in his prophetic statement from the 1800s that race would be *the* issue of the twentieth century. (I posit this was also a lament.) Two decades into the twenty-first century, it still is. If we continue doing things the way we always have, this cancer will continue to consume. Because of its inescapable reality in our lives, people are passionate and highly opinionated about the facets of race in America.

However, if we are truly teachable, not defensive, not easily offended, and not overly committed to a worldview that has perpetuated the problems of race, we can join forces for personal growth and societal change for the better. A good start is to work to make race discussable in the places where you work with others whose race differs from your own.

Resources for Further Learning

Readers should find the following articles helpful:

- "How to Talk About Race in the Workplace," reported by *Aljazeera* https://www.aljazeera.com/features/2019/5/31/how-to-talk-about-race-in-the-workplace
- "How to Have Conversations About Race at Work," reported by *Forbes* https://www.forbes.com/sites/janicegassam/2019/01/28/how-to-have-conversations-about-race-at-work/#6511a5ab5dc5

Declaration of Intent

I commit to help make issues of race discussable in the groups and organizations I participate in by inviting and initiating their discussion, where appropriate, and by welcoming them when raised by other organization members.

_____

Print your name here

_____ Date _____

Sign your name here

Accountability Partner (optional)

I commit that I will share my declaration with _____
and ask him/her to hold me accountable for acting on this declaration.

PRINCIPLE 10

Actively Advocate for Racial Justice and Positive Race Relations

Step 10: Challenge people who show bias in their speech or actions.

Story 1: "Speak Up"

BY DAVID THOMAS

It's difficult for all of us to speak up and risk confrontation or being disliked. For some, it's easier to just go along and be accommodating. There will always be people who choose to be negative and vocal about groups of people who are sometimes defined by race and when that happens, not speaking up is wrong.

I have made it a point in my lifetime to speak up when someone makes derogatory comments about someone's ethnic background or religion. Across the nation in the late '60s, there was much going on related to civil rights, including the elimination of some of the racist laws that existed especially in the South. When I was in college at Michigan State University, a man named George Wallace was running for President of the United States. His platform consisted primarily of maintaining segregation and the Jim Crow laws in the South.

I was on the football team at the time, and many of my teammates were African American. Some were close friends, and we often talked about race. When I saw or heard them smeared with broad, negative comments, I stuck up for them. I still do. I don't even like dumb blond jokes, my wife is a blond.

Over the years, I have developed three ways of letting others know that it is not acceptable to make slanderous comments or jokes about Blacks or offensive remarks regarding other races. They are:

1. Don't smile and act accommodating. Use non-verbal communication to let the offender know you don't approve.
2. Verbally defend your friends. For example, in response to an offensive comment about Blacks I might say, "I have a lot of Black friends. They are good people, and I don't like it when you talk about them or their race." Or I might say, "I don't agree with what you just said;" or "I don't think that joke is funny."
3. I use the following method when I feel exasperated and the effort to have a reasonable discussion seems pointless. The first time I used this method was in college. I was sitting down at lunch with a group of guys, most of whom I didn't know, when one of them talked about voting for George Wallace. After brief bantering back and forth that included a number of objectionable statements, I realized the conversation was going to a bad place. So, I said, "I am not voting for Wallace because my grandfather is Black." It was an obvious untruth, but it terminated the racist talk.

Questions and Steps for Reflection, Discussion, and Further Learning

1. We are all different, and no one approach to challenging racially divisive behavior is best for everyone. How do you think it would be best for you to handle racist or racially derogatory talk?

   _____

   _____

   _____

2. It is often said that perceptions create reality. How does this insight apply to race-related issues in our culture?

   _____

   _____

   _____

3. How do you believe stereotypes (your own or other people's) affect your relationships, especially those with people of another race?

_____

_____

_____

_____

4. Most people believe that when racially offensive comments are made, it is sufficient to do just the first of my three "rules of response,"- don't agree but without a direct challenge. Do you agree? Why or why not?

_____

_____

_____

_____

Author Commentary

The need to be accepted and approved of is something we all want. But this need should not be pursued at the risk of going along with—or indicating approval of—racist thoughts or talk. Being loyal is a virtue as is tolerance of different points of view, but these cannot be maintained at the expense of standing up for right and against wrong. I have been taught that broad, generalized negative comments about a group of people is slander, and slander of any sort is wrong.

Over the years, I have found that speaking up is good for me. As a football player, I learned that the best defense is a good offense. It's best to speak up. Not speaking up is tacitly agreeing with a person. When you hear someone speaking ill of your friend or his race say something. I believe this is a matter of loyalty and morality. One of my favorite quotes is from Tolstoy, who said, "One of the most evil things in the world is when one group of people thinks they are better than another." By not speaking up, we perpetuate this sort of evil.

Story 2: "At the Pro Shop"

BY ANGELO ZERBO

I was in Southern Florida where I own a condo when one day I decided to go to a local driving range and hit some golf balls. As I approached the range, I noticed an older woman getting a lesson from an instructor. After a few minutes of watching the lesson, I was impressed with the techniques the instructor was teaching and how well the student was responding. I knew I needed a lesson and wanted that instructor, who happened to be African American. The range was packed, and the instructor was the only Black man around. The beauty of golf, which Tiger Woods has proven beyond a doubt, is that it is dependent upon skill. Therefore, success in the game is color blind.

Because the pro instructor was in the process of giving a lesson, I went into the pro shop to purchase balls and inquire about him. There were four or five White men in the shop when I asked about the instructor. They asked if I was talking about the Black man. Then they told me he wasn't from there and that I would do much better with one of their instructors, who were all White.

They caught me off guard. The tone and manner of their comments made their implication unmistakable. Before I knew it, I was saying, "I don't care where he's from, and I don't care if he's orange, green, blue or black. The man knows his stuff."

I then went out to where the instructor was teaching, and, when the lesson ended, introduced myself. His name is Bradford Womack. I asked about his availability and booked a lesson which I made clear I wanted to be at that driving range. Later, I made a point of returning and letting the people who were running the driving range and pro shop know I was back to get a lesson from one of the best instructors I had in more than 50 years of playing golf. I hope I left them with a lasting memory and the knowledge that there are all types of people who will not tolerate injustice or racism at any level.

Questions for Reflection, Discussion, and Further Learning

1. Why is it difficult for many of us to verbally challenge speech and behavior that reflects racial bias?

_____

_____

_____

_____

2. Can you think of a time when you were confronted with a similar situation? How did you respond?

_____

_____

_____

_____

3. Most of the stereotypical and prejudiced speech about members of specific racial groups, including Whites, is expressed to members of the speaker's own racial group. Does this fact make Step 10—to challenge people who show bias in their speech or actions—more or less important ? Why ?

_____

_____

_____

_____

Author Commentary

I have learned over time that when a window of opportunity presents itself to right a wrong, we should not hesitate to do something about it. To make change, we must be willing to step up and take a stand.

Resource for Further Learning

The classic film "Gentleman's Agreement," starring Gregory Peck, is an excellent conversation starter and learning tool that deals directly with Step 10.

<u>Declaration of Intent</u>

I will actively advocate for racial justice and positive race relations by, for example, challenging people who show bias in their speech or actions.

_____

Print your name here

_____ Date _____

Sign your name here

Accountability Partner (optional)

I commit that I will share my declaration with _____ and ask him/her to hold me accountable for acting on this declaration.

PRINCIPLE 11

Capitalize on Shared Identities

> **Step 11:** Diffuse racial tension and promote harmony by appealing to broader forms of shared social identity, such as faith, sports team, or organization.

Story: "The Value of Shared Identity"

BY BRADLEY THOMAS

Sometimes the best way to find yourself or feel unique is through interaction with others. Your differences, skills, similarities, and brilliance can shine best when you feel connected to other people. Working together in the boardroom, at the soup kitchen, or on the football field, and connecting with others through shared interests and mutual accomplishments is a foundation of racial unity. Being part of a team can build connections that transcend race.

For me, playing college football at Northwood University in Midland, Michigan, was the best experience of my life. At first, I was apprehensive as I questioned whether my skill set belonged in a Division 1 program. But once we shared the connection and commonality of being on a team, we began to settle in and grow. I did not know much about the real struggles in life for young African Americans until I played college football. I am still good friends with some of the guys I met then, and they changed my life. Our team was diverse, with roughly 50 percent White players and 50 percent Black players. Our hometowns ranged from Pinconning, Michigan, to Fort Lauderdale, Florida. Many of the guys from inner-city Detroit, Grand Rapids, and Flint were my roommates during camp and when we went to travel games. Our connection with football helped us build relationships, allowing us the opportunity to share our thoughts about life and our upbringings. I listened when these guys talked about their struggles. I saw how they didn't have a car or money when others had Suburban's and their parent's credit card. I drove guys home for Christmas and saw where they lived and grew up.

Our coach was a profound influence in terms of promoting positive race relations. Like our team, our coaching staff was racially diverse. If head coach Pat Riepma walked into the campus cafeteria and saw Black guys sitting at one table and White guys at another, he would grab us and make us intersperse with each other. The effect was amazing. He wanted us to be like brothers, and it worked on and off the field. To this day, I maintain many of those relationships. When one of my best friends was recently inducted into Northwood's Hall of Fame, the whole team came together to see it happen. Once again, half of us were White and half of us were Black, but we all felt like brothers.

Questions for Reflection, Discussion, and Further Learning

1. Can you think of an experience you had in which a shared common identity, such as religion, sports, company, or nation helped overcome racial differences and tensions? If so, describe it here.

   _____

   _____

   _____

   _____

2. In the current climate there is considerable polarization based on affiliation with political parties. Why is the common identity as Americans seemingly less relevant, or impactful today than in the past? How could this be changed?

   _____

   _____

3. Sometimes people say things like, "I don't see race. I don't see you as a (fill in the race) person, just as a person." Does this help build positive race relations? Why or why not?

_____

_____

_____

_____

Author Commentary

As we develop in our racial harmony, deliberate collaboration will encourage further growth and strengthen interracial relations. Some of our best relationships are built on the commonality that comes with membership in a social group, whether it be school, sports, work, church, or another group affiliation. If we continue to gather in all White or all Black churches, athletic leagues, and so on, we cannot hope to bridge the racial divide that exists in our nation. Think about your closest relationships and how they were formed. They likely grew out of a social group affiliation. To continue to encourage racial harmony, we must take advantage of common identities that overshadow racial boundaries. We must be willing to put ourselves in situations with people of different races. How else can we begin to learn, understand, and form life-enhancing interracial relationships.

> "…Human beings need three basic things in order to be content: they need to feel competent at what they do; they need to feel authentic in their lives; and they need to feel connected to others."
> – **Sebastian Junger**

Connection to others through common social group memberships can be a springboard to better interracial relations.

Declaration of Intent

When appropriate, I will endeavor to diffuse racial tensions and divisions by appealing to shared social group identities such as faith, sports, or organization.

_____

Print your name here

_____ Date _____

Sign your name here

Accountability Partner (optional)

I commit that I will share my declaration with _____
and ask him/her to hold me accountable for acting on this declaration.

PRINCIPLE 12

Build and Maintain Authentic Interracial Relationships

> **Step 12:** Take specific steps to initiate new, and strengthen existing, associations and friendships with people of different races by, for example, arranging periodic (e.g. monthly) meetings or inviting them to your home.

Story 1: "Remembering Mr. Butts — A Story About Race Relations"
BY HERMAN SHELTON

When I was in the sixth grade, I had a White teacher named Mr. Butts. He was a stocky guy, and because of his name, the kids would make jokes about him. I would often get in trouble from hanging out with these troublemakers. Mr. Butts told me, "There is something good about you. I can see it in you." He said he was going to take me to his house in Royal Oak, Michigan which was essentially an all-White suburb of Detroit at the time. He followed through by teaching me to paint and working me all summer painting.

I remember going to an administrator's house. She said, "Now, don't you tell anybody where I live." Because many people were fearful of a Black kid in a White neighborhood. Mr. Butts didn't care. Throughout the sixth and seventh grades he had me painting all over metro Detroit. He opened up to me and saw something in me as a young African American that others hadn't. As a result I had a White adult who reached out to me when everyone else was doing the opposite. He invited me to his home for dinner with his family, encouraged me to finish my education, and gave me manly principles that my father never gave me. He also gave me a valuable life skill that I could use for the rest of my life.

I thought: " Here is this White man doing this out of his own heart." It had a profound effect on the rest of my life. I have often reflected on the seeds that were planted then, and even though I made mistakes after that, I never felt animosity toward White people because of the interest Mr. Butts took in me.

Questions and Steps for Reflection, Discussion, and Further Learning

1. Is there a person or persons of another race in your past who was especially important in changing your attitudes or beliefs about race? If so, who and how?

   _____

   _____

   _____

2. The fact that this happened to the author very early in his life is significant. What experience, if any, did you have with racial differences and issues during your childhood?

   _____

   _____

   _____

3. Do you have friends, people with whom you interact socially on a regular basis outside of organizational settings, who are from a different racial background? If so, what were the keys to forming and maintaining these relationships? If not, why not?

   _____

   _____

   _____

   _____

Author Commentary

One of the important things to notice in this story is the value of being intentional about forming relationships with people of a different race. Mr. Butts went out of his way to befriend me, despite our differences. Too often racial differences are used as barriers that prevent forming close associations, leaving one with a network of racially homogeneous friends. The story also illustrates how significant it can be for just one person of another race to reach out to someone who is different. As the story points out, I never felt animosity toward White people as a group because of the kindness of this one person.

Story 2: "The Longest Walk Brotherhood"
BY DOMENIC MORELLI

A few years ago my friend Dexter James and I flew to San Francisco to meet a group of Native American people, friends, and supporters to kick off the second leg of a three-year campaign established to stand against domestic violence and drug abuse. The campaign leader was named Dennis Banks (or Nowa Cumig). He was a well-known Native American leader comparable to African American leader, Dr. Martin Luther King Jr. Dennis was a peaceful man who stood for causes that brought people together to fight against injustice. One of the slogans he shared was, "One People, One Planet."

A new friend and brother, Ray St. Clair, who was one of Dennis's right-hand people invited us to a gathering that helped assemble people and resources and cast the vision for a major event called the "Longest Walk." That year, the event started near the Golden Gate Bridge and walkers and runners pushed toward Washington, D.C. where the walk comes to a close in front of the Lincoln Memorial. During the few days we gathered in San Francisco our Native American brothers and sisters held prayer time and drum and peace-pipe ceremonies.

We felt honored to be a part of this intimate setting, where each person stood against injustice and gathered as One People, One Planet. During the first peace-pipe ceremony, Dexter James, an African American pastor from Detroit, was the only non-native invited to participate. I was excited to see my friend receive this honor.

Ray explained that Natives normally don't invite White people to join the ceremony because of the way the Whites have treated the Native Americans over many years. "The White people have not kept any treaties that they have made with the Native Americans. We empathize with African Americans because we have both been abused by Whites. The African Americans were abused through slavery, and we have been abused by Whites taking our land while killing and abusing our people," he said.

Hearing my brother Ray share how Whites have hurt Native People and people of my friend Dexter's racial group struck my heart. I realized my brotherhood with Ray and Dennis was the only reason I was invited to attend the "Longest Walk." And I grasped that it was my friendship with Pastor Dexter that led us to join this event in support of our brother Ray. We all came together through a loving and supportive relationship in the spirit of "One People, One Planet."

The next day, as the walk continued from San Francisco, I had the opportunity to meet many more Native leaders, and Ray was able to share the bond between Pastor Dexter, Dennis, myself and him with everyone on the walk. On the next scheduled ceremony stop Chief Wounded Knee started with a drum ceremony and prayer followed by a peace-pipe ceremony, each in honor of the ancestors and to bless the walk. Since Ray shared the closeness of our brotherhood, the group invited me to participate in the pipe ceremony. I couldn't stop thinking about how, for so many years, Native and African Americans have endured various forms of oppression due in part to actions by the White majority. Yet, despite this history, they accepted me as one of their brothers.

Questions for Reflection, Discussion, and Further Learning:

1. To what extent have you thought about the social and economic struggles of Native and African Americans?

   _____

   _____

   _____

   _____

2. How has expansion and economic development in the United States impacted different racial groups (in similar and contrary ways)?

_____

_____

_____

3. Do you have social relationships with people who are of different racial or ethnic groups? If so, how have these relationships changed your views or enriched you?

_____

_____

_____

4. The story reveals how many Native Americans are still affected by the Anglo-Native American relations that unfolded over hundreds of years. This also applies to White and African American relations. However, many feel we should just "get over this ancient history." What is your view of this? _____

_____

_____

_____

5. What does the story teach about relating to people as individuals rather than as members of a social identity group?

_____

_____

_____

Author Commentary

It was eye opening to see and hear the perspectives of my brother Ray and other Native people regarding White-Native relations over many years and of their empathy for African Americans who endured pain through slavery and continued mistreatment. As I was growing up and became a young man, very little of this information was on my radar.

What brought this so close to my heart was a true love for my brothers, who are of a different race than me, and coming to understand that much of the pain racial minorities endured was caused by White people. As a White person, I feel honored to be their brother and to be accepted into their family. I do look at my journey very differently as I learned the term "One People, One Planet" from Dennis Banks and I look forward to our continued journey together.

Although the story I presented here is about my relationships with Native Americans, I believe the message of the value of forming genuine friendships with people of different races is applicable to all interracial scenarios.

Declaration of Intent

I will endeavor to establish and maintain authentic relationships and friendships with a racially diverse mix of people.

_____

Print your name here

_____ Date _____

Sign your name here

Accountability Partner (optional)

I commit that I will share my declaration with _____ and ask him/her to hold me accountable for acting on this declaration.

ABOUT THE AUTHORS

Taylor Cox Jr.

Taylor Cox Jr. is an internationally known writer and organizational consultant. He is founder and chief executive officer of Taylor Cox and Associates, a research and consulting firm specializing in the assessment and change of organizational culture and in assisting organizations with the challenges and opportunities of culturally diverse workforces and markets. He is also founding pastor of Living the Word Christian Ministries of Hazel Park, Michigan. He holds Bachelor of Science and Master of Business Administration degrees from Wayne State University and a Ph.D. in business administration from The University of Arizona.

During a twenty-year career as an academic, Taylor served as a faculty member and administrator at several universities, including Duke University, Winston Salem State University, The University of North Carolina at Charlotte, and The University of Michigan, where he earned tenure in 1995. His teaching in business schools has included a wide range of topics including small business management, organizational strategy, human resource management, manufacturing strategy, and statistics. He has published extensively and won multiple awards, including the Best Book Award from the National Academy of Management for his book *Cultural Diversity in Organizations: Theory, Research & Practice*. He and his wife, Cynthia, live in West Bloomfield, Michigan.

Shannon Gaston

As a skilled practitioner, consultant, and speaker, Shannon Gaston is widely considered one of Detroit's most dynamic youth development leaders. His passion and commitment to young people is evidenced by two decades of service in which he has impacted more than 5,000 youth in Detroit, Michigan; Kenya; Ethiopia; and Jamaica.

He is currently director of Young Life-Detroit, a non-denominational Christian organization devoted to reaching adolescents in the area. Shannon is responsible for building relationships, managing volunteers and staff, and executing club meetings and camping trips. He is also a member of the organization's Urban Elders team, which supports regional leaders and staff in diversity efforts that include the attraction and retention of staff of color.

Shannon holds a bachelor degree in biology from Wayne State University and a masters degree in intercultural and urban studies from Moody Bible Institute. As an emerging scholar, Shannon's research is focused on exploring cross-cultural opportunities for shared power, indigenous leadership development, and building authentic relationships in the context of urban ministry. Shannon, his wife and children live in Detroit, Michigan.

Dexter James

Dexter James is founder and senior pastor of Inner-City Outreach Ministries of Detroit, Michigan and founder and president of The Rainbow Fellowship Center of Decatur, Georgia. He is also founder of The Miller Wright Men's Fellowship Home in Detroit. His mission is to help community members in need of support build solid spiritual and economic foundations for themselves and their families. His work focuses on assisting men from poor socio-economic backgrounds whose lives are off track to get a fresh start. His organizations provide assistance with housing, job training, and biblical teaching. During the past seventeen years, his Inner-City Outreach men's home and other organizations helped transform the lives of hundreds of men.

Domenic Morelli

Domenic Morelli was born on Detroit's Eastside where he attended St. Jude School. He then moved to Southgate and attended St. Frances Cabrini High School, from which he graduated in 1978.

He was trained in the family construction business where he saw a need for higher-caliber roofing products. Domenic entered the roofing and coating industry in 1979. He is one of the original pioneers of Modified Bitumen Roofing Products, importing materials from Europe while assisting with education and helping build some of the first manufacturing plants in Texas and New Jersey. He has been involved in energy savings programs since the early 1990's and was a charter member of Energy Star in the roofing industry.

Domenic has served as a guest speaker for the Roof Consultants Institute in Texas, Alaska, Arkansas, and Ontario, Canada, presenting on environmentally friendly, sustainable, green, and cool roofing products with solar and daylighting. He has presented to hundreds of architectural organizations on the benefits of energy-saving products and services, written several articles published in *Contractors Guide* and the *Florida Forum*, and has been quoted in the popular magazine *Roofing Contractor*. As past president of Tri-Ply Roofing Products and executive vice president of Thermo Materials, Domenic developed knowledge in all aspects of commercial roofing throughout North America.

A follower of Jesus, Domenic serves on the Board of Faith Works Michigan and Youth with a Mission Metro Detroit, where he tries to do the things Jesus would do in supporting family and community. He is also a conduit for uniting the city and the suburbs through Metro Detroit nonprofits, including Life Remodeled, HOPE, and Inner City Outreach Ministries and through other companies, individual supporters, and organizations to create jobs and opportunities for the next generation of Detroiters. Domenic and his wife, Verna, live in the Detroit Metro Area. They have four children and nine grandchildren.

Nico Meylan

Nico Meylan is founder and director of Youth With A Mission (YWAM) Metro Detroit. A native of Switzerland who spent ten years traveling the world as a missionary and speaker, he is passionate about bringing together people of diverse backgrounds and ethnicities. He lives in Detroit with his wife, Marley.

Terrence Oprea

Terry Oprea is an award-winning marketing and media veteran who has spent nearly 40 years in the marketing and news industries. He is former owner, president, and CEO of integrated marketing firm MCCI (Mort Crim Communications, Inc.), which he sold at the end of 2019.

About 70 percent of MCCI's revenue comes from publicly and privately held, national and global firms.

Oprea began building the firm from the ground up 26 years ago with his then-partner Mort Crim. At MCCI, Terry took a front seat in the amazing transition from a print and broadcast-based media and marketing culture to one that heavily depends on digital communications. The firm has more than sixty awards for its expertise in integrated marketing communications, content development, and media messaging.

Terry has trained or given strategic counsel to scores of corporate executives, government leaders, and marketing/sales professionals in the art of effective communications, messaging, and marketing. Clients have included major banking institutions, health care systems, global manufacturing firms, utilities, consumer product organizations, government entities, universities, and others.

His career has included positions as executive producer at Post-Newsweek Television, news editor at Time-Life Broadcasting, vice president for National Programming at WTVS public television, and NBC state supervisor in Indiana for NBC News Elections.

Terry has received numerous awards for excellence, including the American Bar Association's prestigious Silver Gavel award, a National Headliner Award; UPI's top national award, two first-place national Angel awards, the Crystal Communicator Award of Excellence, six regional Emmy awards, and other accolades. Terry is still active in serving his national and international clientele as well as serving on the board of multiple nonprofit organizations.

James Rose Jr.

James (Jim) Rose serves as global managing director of Client Services for all Deloitte member service firms to the Ford Motor Company. He is responsible for delivering the firm's multi-disciplinary solutions, which include business, innovation, and IT consulting as well as privacy, enterprise risk management, tax, and financial advisory services.

With more than twenty years of experience, Jim's career has been accentuated by leading-edge projects that assist automotive manufacturing companies with innovative technology and business performance improvement. His skill set includes corporate strategy, mergers and acquisitions, supply-chain optimization, automotive aftermarket, marketing, information technology, and new product development. He is distinguished within his firm as a Deloitte CIO Fellow and was recently honored with the Deloitte Innovator of the Year Award.

In addition to Ford, Jim has serviced many leading automotive original equipment manufacturers. Prior to joining Deloitte, he worked as an advanced engineering director for Tata Technologies and held executive management positions with Carlisle & Company, Blue Titan Software, OEConnection, Xerox, and IBM.

Jim holds a Bachelor of Arts in music performance from the New England Conservatory of Music and did post-graduate study at The Julliard School of Music. He is also a graduate of the IBM Executive Education program of the University of Warwick in England with a concentration in Marketing.

Herman Shelton Jr.

Herman Shelton Jr. is founder and chief executive officer of Right Choices, a nonprofit devoted to coaching youth and families as they deal with difficult situations, and to promoting the making of positive life choices. He is widely recognized as a motivational speaker and community leader in Metro Detroit. Using his own life story and testimony of life transformation, Herman inspires young men and women to make decisions that will improve their opportunities for success. He is a strong advocate for education and consistently promotes lifelong learning, personal responsibility, and love for self and others. Working in schools and speaking in conferences, he has reached thousands of young people and their families throughout the U.S.

Bradley Thomas

Brad Thomas is a certified financial planner in Bloomfield Hills, Michigan. His practice focuses on income planning for people who are at or near retirement. Brad attended De La Salle Collegiate High School in Macomb County, Michigan, where he earned a football scholarship to Northwood University in Midland. He was a three-time, all-GLIAC, all-academic player and graduated with a bachelor degree in business administration.

Brad volunteers with the Detroit Humane Society and the Downtown Boxing Gym in Detroit. For the latter, he tutors youth in math and English weekly as part of an award-winning program. His interactions with the youth have had a profound effect on his life. Injustice in corporate, economic, and criminal justice systems has weighed heavily on Brad's mind and actions. He believes the group authoring this book has found a way to have a real, sustainable impact. Although he was initially skeptical about joining the group, Brad found that it enabled him and his counterparts to grow and learn. He wants to share that learning with others. His great hope and expectation are that this book will be a catalyst toward positive change. He resides in Huntington Woods with his wife, Janessa, and their two dogs.

David Thomas

Dave Thomas and his two oldest sons, Bradley and Joseph, founded Thomas Financial Co. in 2009. They serve their clients as investment advisors and wealth managers.

Dave has been in the financial service industry since graduating from Michigan State University, where he was part of the most integrated football team in the country—one nationally ranked in the Top 2 in the mid- to late-1960s. As a player, he learned to respect and value his teammates and has maintained many of those friendships. He enjoys listening to and learning about and from people. His friends, especially his African American friends, the books he has read, and his faith have helped form his thoughts about life, Blacks, Whites, and race relations. David has been married to Janis for more than forty years. They have seven adult children and five grandchildren.

Rick Warren

Rick Warren is chairman and chief executive officer of Weldaloy Specialty Forgings Co., where he has been sole shareholder since 1994. He received a Bachelor of Science in finance from Michigan State University. Throughout his career, he has launched and led accounting, real estate development, and management consulting firms.

Amid his entrepreneurship and business enterprises, Rick's true passions are for people and the gospel. He is heavily involved with various ministries and nonprofit organizations around the country, many of which support education. To learn more about Rick, his story, and his charitable and community activity, visit <u>TheOtherRickWarren.com</u>.

Angelo Zerbo

Angelo Zerbo was born and raised in Detroit, Michigan. He is a lifelong entrepreneur who has founded and grown businesses in several industries. For the past 34 years, he has worked as owner and chief executive officer of A&Z Commercial Roofing, a highly successful business located in Farmington Hills, Michigan.

This publication is a project of the Alliance for Racial Harmony. For further information or to donate please go to our web site at racial-harmony.org.

Printed in the United States
By Bookmasters